Musings from Fourth Place

THOMAS F. SLEETE

© Copyright 2019 Thomas F. Sleete. All rights reserved.

Book Cover:
Photo by Channing Jones
Design by Anabel Bouza

Layout:
Rachel Greene for elfinpen designs

ISBN 13: 978-1-947153-09-7
ISBN 10: 1-947153-09-9

This book is dedicated to my grandchildren, present and future. It is also dedicated to all those who, like me, have lost a spouse or loved one and whose grief is ongoing.

Fabula Est Vestri
(The Story is Yours)

"I would give anything I own
Give up my life, my heart, my home
I would give everything I own
Just to have you back again
Just to touch you once again"

BREAD (LYRICS BY DAVID GATES)

Acknowledgements

First and foremost, I thank Jesus Christ, my Lord and Savior. Without Him, there is no way I that I would have made it even this far since Moe's passing.

My family are the ones for whom I originally composed this book, in order to show them how I have continued to deal with the loss of the woman we all loved so dearly, and to provide more insight into just who their father was and is. For being who they are they have my profound thanks, pride, and love.

Special thanks to my son, Tyson, for his proofreading, editing, and invaluable suggestions.

I sincerely thank Pastor David Stokes, who continues to provide wise guidance and direction in order for me to get this project into print.

My deepest thanks to my dear friends and counselors Joe Brandell and Pastor Stan Rayford along with the other pastors in my life, Chris Hodges, Ike Hendershot, Phil Bassham, Beau McCarthy, and Nate Sjrogen.

Finally, this is for you, Moe. Forever by my side. I love you Babe. Always have. Always will. See you soon.

"Living in the light of eternity changes your priorities."

RICK WARREN

Why Fourth Place?

When I was an adolescent, I remember visiting the home of my favorite cousins. As I was hanging out one day, I noticed a plaque above one of my cousins' bed. It read, "I'm Third."

Finding that an odd thing to look at every day, I asked my cousin what it meant. He replied, "It's simple really. What it means is that in my life, God is first, others are second, and I'm third."

The more I thought about it, the more sense it made to me. What a great way to prioritize what is truly important in one's life. I was so impressed, I began to try to live by it.

As I've gotten older, I've found that my life has been dedicated to the philosophy that should really read, "I'm Fourth." If I am honest in how I've tried to arrange the relationships in my life, I've had to revise the old saying. For me, God is still first, my family is second, others are third, and I'm fourth.

The second great commandment, according to Jesus Christ, who knew a thing or two about them, is to love your neighbor as yourself. Believe me, I've tried. Early on I failed miserably. Those who irritated me, annoyed me, offended me, opposed me, and otherwise became a pain in my....posterior, were not loved.

However, as I've matured, I've come to realize that loving others as I love myself isn't really that hard. If one is truly honest, and not consumed by narcissism, one can admit that they are not all that overwhelmingly lovable in the first place. One of my children asked me if loving others means we also have to like them, and I answered that I didn't think that was mandatory. After all, Jesus came to save everyone, even the Pharisees whose actions He despised. But He loved them as He loved everyone else. In short, I find it much easier to adhere to my being in fourth place.

And, here's the cool part. In baseball, the fourth place hitter bats cleanup and is always the most valuable and powerful hitter in the lineup. So there.

On Grieving

PART ONE

"My pain is either a jail that imprisons me or a school that shapes me."

PASTOR CHRIS HODGES

The Path I Took

Pastor Chris Hodges of Church of the Highlands, in collaboration with Pastor Rick Warren of Saddleback Church, delivered a message on surviving life's worst moments. In it he elaborated six steps that can, but not always, be the path to overcoming the worst that life has to offer. I've expressed before, in my previous book, my lack of use for the Kubler-Ross "stages of grief". In my case I found them to not be applicable.

However, the six steps that Pastor Chris explained rang true to my experience. As I listened to the message, I found myself saying, with each passing, "Yep. Been there, done that." When I lost my wife, Moe, to her heart attack on January 20, 2017, I was emotionally devastated. It came out of nowhere and hurled me to the figurative ground. Through the grace of God, I've been able to survive. Wounded, scarred, and forever missing her, I continue on until that glorious day when I will see her again. That being said, here are the six steps and the impact they had on me.

Shock. This one is, obviously, the easiest to explain. When I watched the love of my life die while I was holding her hand, anguish and desolation are insufficient to express how staggered I was. I couldn't comprehend, or even believe, what had just happened. After two weeks in the cardiac intensive care unit, she seemed to be making progress. We were talking and she was finally sitting up in a chair next to me when, without warning, she died. It was disbelief like I've never experienced.

Sorrow. This is one that, as far as I'm concerned, never fully leaves my heart. I miss her and I still love her. The hole in my heart will never be filled by anything or anyone in this life. So many descriptive words and phrases come to mind, but that would be a waste of space. Simply put, for a time it is all-encompassing and seemingly unendurable.

Struggle. As I dealt with the sorrow, I struggled to get my bearings. There was so much to try to understand and to deal with. I had to try to grasp the answer to the simplest of questions, "Why?" To paraphrase Pascal, there will always be a Moe-sized vacuum in my emotions. But having those with whom I could share this burden, eased it to a great degree. My children, my brother, my sister-in-law, my pastors and my friends, all shared in it and prayed for me in my grief. That is quite an array of comfort.

Surrender. The most spiritually significant moments came when I decided to get off the throne and give all of the grief to God. I knew that I couldn't deal with the shattered shards of my heart. I gave it all to Him. I knew from the moment that she died that He was with me. He never let me go. And I let go and I yielded it all to Him. What a release and easing of a seemingly indomitable foe within me. I went from feeling like an emotional Custer to a bloodied and bowed conqueror.

Sanctification. No, this does not mean that I became perfect. What it means is that I learned the lessons that this kind of grief teaches. Churchill once said, "I am always ready to learn although I do not always like being taught." In this case, I could not agree more. Through this refining fire I came to understand grief, the pain of others, the loneliness of loss, and so much more. It is a hard-won perspective and one that is never forgotten.

Service. I knew that I wanted to use this entire process to hopefully provide a lifeline for others. So, I wrote a blog, which became the book titled *"Handling Grief: A Christian's Ongoing Journey with Loss."* I am awed by how the Lord guided me to write it and, most of all, how so many have expressed to me their thankfulness for it and the impact it had on them. No matter how it was acquired, it has, at the very least, provided some form of help to others, while honoring Moe. I say this not to sell books, (I've given away far more than have been sold) just to show that was my goal and, I pray, it was also His.

Will everyone go through these steps? Definitely not. But I provide it as one man's experience with what the pastors provided.

> *"My most brilliant achievement was my ability to persuade my wife to marry me."*
>
> WINSTON CHURCHILL

7 - 8 - 7 - 8

Moe and I were married on July 8th, 1978, in the most beautiful church in the Detroit area. On that day, her Dad told me that I should buy a lottery ticket. I asked if that was because I was so fortunate to be marrying his daughter and he said it was because the numbers 7/8/78 sounded like winners. He and I laughed about that through the years because those numbers were definitely not lottery winners that day.

But I was the ultimate winner.

I must confess to a checkered career when it comes to our anniversaries. Of course we always acknowledged them and celebrated to some degree, but as the years passed I would occasionally mess up. As an example, in 2003 my family and all of Moe's family (parents, five brothers and sisters plus spouses and children) were celebrating my son's graduation from high school, in La Jolla, California. One day, my brother-in-law and I decided to take all of the assembled kids to a San Diego Padres game. We left the "women folk" back at the hotel and went to the game. In about the third inning, I looked at the scoreboard and realized it was July 8th, 2003, our 25th anniversary! I immediately borrowed a cell phone and called Moe. She laughed so hard at me and told me she was waiting for me to realize the date. Of course, I already had a gift for her, but I hadn't said a word about the significance of the day that morning. She told me that all was forgiven due to the fact that we had taken all of the kids and it gave her time to be alone with her beloved sisters.

Whew!

As the years rolled on, I was often out of town doing workshops for various universities or the College Board on our anniversary. Moe always said that the day didn't matter since we both knew how much we loved each other every day.

And then, this past July, the poignant date arrived. July 8th, 2018 would have been our 40th anniversary.

Forty years and here I was, without her. So many thoughts and emotions engendered turbulence in my soul. How I missed her every day, how much I loved and love her still, how I wish she could be here to see our children and how they've become such wonderful adults, how much she is missed by our five year old granddaughter and what a breathtakingly marvelous little girl she has become, how much I need her to be with me, how she is always in my thoughts, and on and on.

Heartbreaking, tender, moving, distressing. It was all of those and then some. But, as is always the case in my life, the Lord threw me lifelines. The first is the sure knowledge that, in what to her will seem such a short time, we will be together again in His presence.

The second is found in Hebrews 12:1. It tells of how we are surrounded by a "great cloud of witnesses". I like to believe that Moe is in the crowd, and though she can't see the bad that happens because that would be counterintuitive to the perfection of the Lord's presence, she can see the good. And there is an abundance of that.

So I said aloud, "Happy Anniversary, Babe. I'll see you soon."

And I was at peace.

"This is one of the miracles of love: It gives a power of seeing through its own enchantments and yet not being disenchanted."

C. S. LEWIS

A Miracle

I overheard someone saying that in order for someone to find the perfect mate, they had to find someone who had the same interests, philosophies, and beliefs. When I heard it the only thought that went through my mind was, "What a crock!"

If either Moe or I had thought that way, we never would have married or shared a love that is to be envied. When we met, we were so different in so many ways. Herewith a baker's dozen examples.

She was into cool jazz and I loved heavy metal.

She preferred seafood and I was a meat and potatoes guy.

Moe had a Corvette and I had a Harley-Davidson.

She was raised a Roman Catholic and I was raised a Southern Baptist.

Moe was an artist and art teacher while I was a history teacher and history geek.

She wasn't into sports, I loved sports and played three of them.

When she slept, she completely covered herself except for her feet and I slept with no covers on except for the part that covered my feet.

She was more liberal politically and I was more conservative.

Moe was beautiful and I was not about to be cast as the romantic lead in a movie.

She loved coffee and I had never had even one cup of the stuff.

Moe knew, after our first date, that there was something special about us as a couple and I took a short while to get to that point.

She came from a large family in which she had five brothers and sisters while I had only one sibling, my brother.

Moe was right-brained and I was left-brained.

In other words, had a casino become aware of those facts, they'd have issued long odds on our ever being a couple that would last. But we did. From the moment we met to the day she went home to be with the Lord, we had just short of 40 years together.

I could trot out all of the embedded wisdom as an example of why we made it. Opposites attract. When a couple is created, the two become one with each making up half of the whole and each making up for the shortcomings of the other.

I see the astuteness of those, but in my mind, they fall far short of why we fell in love with each other. It's very simple, it was a miracle that I did not earn but with which I was blessed for eternity. God looked down and joined us together knowing just what He was doing.

Was our life together all sunshine, lollipops, and perpetual bliss? Of course not. Life threw just as many virtual beanball pitches at our heads as it did to anyone. Deaths of family and friends, the rigors of parenthood, disagreements on mostly minor issues, and so on. But, through it all, our love never wavered. I remember that once, in a store, Moe was engaged in a conversation with a cashier. The woman commented on the fact that we had been married so long. Moe said to her, "You want to know the cool part? Not only do I love him, but I also still like him." Kind of captures it all as far as I'm concerned.

One of Moe's favorite songs was performed by Curtis Stigers, and written by Barry Mann and Stigers. It is called Never Saw a Miracle. One of the first lines in it both personifies, and expresses, what I felt the first time I laid eyes on the love of my life. *"Never saw a miracle, 'til baby I found you."*

And that moment led to a life together overflowing with little miracles for which I will always be so thankful.

So, if you're looking for the perfect match, don't pay attention to the lists of qualifications that others may make for you. Just be open to letting God prod you in the right direction. As I've always said, the Lord does not crack a door open on opportunity, He slams it open so that it can't be missed.

> *"There are some people who have the quality of richness and joy in them and they communicate it to everything they touch. It is first of all a physical quality; then it is a quality of the spirit."*

TOM WOLFE

Joy and Touch

Mark Twain couldn't have been more wrong when he wrote that there is no joy in heaven. Even a cursory Biblical study of heaven reveals nothing but joy there. I pity his lack of understanding.

One of the talents I had was my ability to make Moe laugh. And did we ever laugh in our years together. It wouldn't take much to spur our bouts of guffawing, and so much of the hilarity was just between us. However, on occasion, it would become public. What follows are two examples of our unashamed enjoyment of humor.

One night many years ago, Moe and I went to a Barnes and Noble to look for books to read. We were an aisle apart when Moe said to me, "Tom, look. They have books on CD for the deaf. (Of course, she meant the blind.) I told her that I knew that and had heard the CD version of the Bible for the deaf. I then cupped my hands over my mouth and, at the top of my lungs, shouted, "IN THE BEGINNING, GOD CREATED THE HEAVENS AND THE EARTH!!!" Moe knew the goof she had made and knew that I was milking it for all I was able. Add to that the attention we had gotten from staff and customers, and we could not stop laughing. At least we weren't thrown out that time.

On another occasion, we decided to go out to dinner, just the two of us. We went to a little restaurant in a strip mall. When we arrived, a bit before 5:00 PM, we saw that the establishment was closed until 5:00. So, we stood at the door and talked. Two other couples showed up, and got in line behind us. A couple minutes before five, a man and woman arrived in their extremely expensive car. He was what I would have described and what I perceived to be an older wealthy self-important businessman, country club and jet set type, along with his younger adult female companion. Seeing the line at the door, and also seeing the sign on the door, he nevertheless went to the door and tried to open it. Being the smart aleck I am, I immediately said out loud, "Oh thank you! We're a parade of incredibly stupid people who have been waiting for someone to come along and try the door to see if the restaurant is really not open." Moe began to laugh out loud, as did the other four in line. "Skipper", as I named him to Moe, was ticked, but with six people laughing at this folly, he retreated to his luxurious car and waited until we all got into the restaurant.

By the way, the other two men who had been waiting each told me that they wished they had thought of and said what I did.

I must, though, write about another kind of joy that far surpasses the elation and delight of making the one you love laugh. That is the joy of touch. I can still feel Moe's hand in mine even though she's been gone for just over two years. I can distinctly remember specific and general occasions when we touched.

When I rewired a wall lamp in the bathroom of our first house and Moe insisted on holding my hand as I prepared to turn on the light. She said that if I was going to be electrocuted, she was definitely going with me.

As she gave birth to all three of our children and when we saw our granddaughter for the first time.

In church and while singing praise songs.

Whenever we walked together in public.

When we said good night to each other.

And for no reason at all, just to touch.

A musician named Dan Hill wrote one of our favorite songs titled "Sometimes When We Touch". He wrote of how in their touch the honesty was too much, how he wanted to hold her till he died and their touch would make them both break down and cry.

His lyrics express, so much more eloquently that I can, how much I miss her touch and the sheer joy it brought to this simple man. But the tears he mentions would be tears of joy for Moe and for me.

"All the lonely people, where do they all come from?"

THE BEATLES

Alone vs. Lonely

I am quite often told by individuals that I certainly don't look 71 years old. My usual reply is, "Thank you, but you should see it from in here", as I point to my heart. What I want to say is that in my opinion, they are right. I don't look a day over 70.

What my age brings me is a perspective that has become vibrant in these past few years. I observe things that I used to ignore and often want to interject myself into situations. For example, I went out to breakfast with my good friend Joe Brandell the other day. As we were leaving we were preceded by a couple, probably in their late 50s or early 60s. He held the door for his wife for a second but since she was adjusting her scarf, he let it close on her to the point that it almost hit her in the face. He, instead, kept on walking to the car and opened his door and didn't open hers.

I wanted to go up to him and, after smacking him in the face for the contempt he'd shown his wife, tell him how lucky he was to still have her in his life. How she deserved his respect and love even though his behavior showed that he was a self-important boor.

But, I didn't. You see, I had seen them in the restaurant and they were one of those couples who eat together, but don't say a word to each other throughout the meal. Together, yet alone. I pity them.

I've also noticed so many people around my age sitting alone in places. Church, theaters, restaurants, shopping centers, bookstores, and other locations. That has made me think that there are a lot of lonely people out there. Ones who seem to have no one else with whom to accompany them to these sites.

And I feel for them. In my heart I want to comfort them, engage in conversation with them. I want to tell them that they don't have to be lonesome. But that means that I would be assuming that they are lonely and not just alone by their own choice.

In this day and age of telephone absorption and social media, it is a wonder to me that so many seem to be going at life single-handedly. It seems as if it is a condition of those who are older, rather than the ones whose daily lives are tethered to the media and electronic gadgetry of modern technology.

As I've said many times before, I quite often am alone but I am NEVER lonely. I have the Lord with whom I can and do talk. I have memories of Moe. I am blessed to have family with whom I can interact and converse. Friends and neighbors are also there for me. But, as must we all, I try to make a conscious effort to retain these links and exchanges.

I believe that from now on, when I feel prodded by the Holy Spirit to speak to someone who is alone and seemingly not enjoying it, I will try to strike up a brief conversation. Without seeming creepy, of course. If and when I do, I'll leave them with the following verses from Psalm 68: 5-6

"A father to the fatherless, a defender of widows, is God in His holy dwelling. God sets the lonely in families, he leads out the prisoners with singing; but the rebellious live in a sun-scorched land."

I'll tell them that there are all kinds of families and there are also all kinds of self-imposed prisons from which we must be released. Then, if they want to hear more of the gospel, I will gladly share it.

A line from Three Dog Night resonates. *"One is the loneliest number that you'll ever do."*

How I Got to Here

"Kind words do not cost much. Yet they accomplish much."

BLAISE PASCAL

How I Got to Here

As I mentioned before, my Dad was a pastor. He wrote the following.

"To every life there comes a day, hour, time; its moments of joy, hours of languid suffering, of affliction, poignant circumstances.

To every man the cup is passed and each in turn drink therefrom.

Life is made up of its mountain peaks and its valleys, all of which form life's burdens.

Some lives are completely overwhelmed by them.

Others succeed in overwhelming.

When the hour comes to man to face them all in their dreadful reality, then to him is the crisis.

The crisis, in turn, reveals the man, his fortitude and his foundation."

My Dad was married in the late 1920s to a woman from his church. They conceived six children, none of whom survived. Three were miscarried and three were still-born.

As time went on, as my Dad told me, they both fell out of love. He then had a decision to make. Should he continue to serve Jesus as a pastor, or remain married and living a lie. He chose divorce.

Keep in mind this was in the 1930s, in Covington KY, and he was a pastor in a Southern Baptist Church. Still, the church kept him as pastor and he did not date or go out with another woman until his ex-wife passed away. In 1946, he married my Mom. In 1947 she gave birth to me and seven years later to my brother. God had honored my father's wish for sons because he had done God's will in his personal life.

Fast forward to 1970. My father died that year when I was just 23 and my brother was one month from 16. I spoke at his funeral and it was the most difficult speech I ever delivered. Both my brother and I loved, and still love him so.

In early 1973, I attended a service at my father's former church. I can honestly say that I did not care for the new pastor. Remembering this era, I was a long haired, bearded, young man. I rode a Harley-Davidson and was a public school history teacher.

After the service ended, a woman approached me in the sanctuary. I had known her for my entire life and was friends with her daughter. She pulled me aside and I, foolishly and happily, greeted her. She fixed me with a cross stare and then said, "I just want you to know that you are a disgrace to your father's memory." Not because I wasn't a Christian. Not because I had caused any kind of scandal. Because of the way I looked.

Being in a fragile emotional state, I abandoned church. For years. I didn't want anything to do with those judgmental so-called Christians. I never stopped believing in Jesus, I simply put him on the back burner. And in the interest of being honest, I plunged headlong into a life outside of God's will. All because that woman, with a hardened heart, had said the words I needed to jump off the emotional bridge.

Three years later, I fell on my knees at my bedside, having just sinned to an extreme that convicted me and for which I needed forgiveness. But I could not forgive myself. Lost, I traveled to California to see a college friend. She was a dynamic Christian and wonderful person. I confessed all I'd done and told her what I felt about forgiveness. Her name is Nancy, and this is the genius-level thing she did. She got up from the table where we were sitting and got her Bible. She set it down in front of me and issued a challenge. She said, "Go ahead and find it. I have all night." I asked her what I was to find. She replied, "Find the verse or verses that say that you can't be forgiven for what you've done. Go ahead, find them."

Of course, there aren't any. The Lord and the angels rejoice at a repentant sinner. And here I was wallowing in doubt. Nancy's words and challenge had freed me.

I tell this story in order to emphasize the power of our words. The evil that was unleashed by me after the hurtful words by that woman, and the wonderful healing that I relished when Nancy brought me to my senses as a Christian.

Choose your words carefully, you never know what impact they may have. Always remember that it wasn't the sinners who wanted to crucify Jesus, it was the self-righteous.

"I've always been crazy, it's kept me from going insane."

WAYLON JENNINGS

History Maker

As a boy, I was shy. Oh, I had my friends in the neighborhood, but when it came to meeting new people, especially adults. I was very uncomfortable.

Painfully so.

But, once in school, I learned a couple of things that got me through. The first is that I can be a pretty funny guy. The second and most important was the fact that humor provides a buffer for the insecure. A place behind which we can hide our true self.

In high school I was accepted by all levels of 1960s high school social strata. Greasers, frats, nerds, jocks, everyone. Let's face it, who doesn't like to laugh? Maturing, I retained my humor and continued to use it as a protective shield.

In college, I started changing. I recently went to a gathering of some of my fraternity brothers from college. One of them said, "You know, Tom, we all believe that you had the biggest misnomer for a nickname in the fraternity. After all, we called you

"Saint", and you were far from it. True, you were a hilarious true friend, but dude, you were NOT a saint."

After graduation, at the height of the Vietnam War, I was classified 1-A for the draft by the Selective Service System. It was 1969 and it was the first year in which they implemented the draft lottery. If drafted, I would have served, but my birthday got the number 345, far higher than the number 195 which was the highest called to serve that year. And all I can ask is, why was I not chosen?

When I graduated and started my teaching career, I roomed with a good friend. We lived in an old house in which he had grown up, down a dirt road with only two houses on it. My roommate, Jim, had a friend named Albert. Albert was an amazing character. He was the pound for pound strongest man I've ever known and he was the nastiest and most accomplished fighter I ever saw. He had served some time in jail for theft and had a larcenous streak in himself that was light years long.

One night, as we were having a party at the house, Albert pulled Jim aside. He said, "Jim, you know me. You know what I am and who I am. I fear nothing. But I want to tell you something. I really like your roommate Tom but, I gotta tell you, that man is crazy. Capital C crazy."

None of that is bragging. I give you all of this in order to teach a lesson. Charles Haddon Spurgeon laid it out perfectly when he wrote, "Whenever God means to make a man great, He always breaks him in pieces first." If you substitute the word "useable" for "great" in that sentence, I think you could provide my picture for its poster.

God broke me but good. In waves it came. My father died. A young woman and I sinned egregiously. I had a motorcycle accident and then a car accident in which another out of control car used my car, standing at a light, as a ramp to vault over and crash into another. I fell asleep behind the wheel of my car while on the expressway and awoke just in time to swerve into a curve. I don't know, do you think he was trying to get my attention? My guardian angel(s) were getting overtime pay and emergency leave for R and R.

And He brought me to my knees. I wept. I prayed for forgiveness and repented. I sought counsel from dear friends in the faith. I once heard that true holiness is abandonment. So, I finally surrendered ALL of my life to Him.

And waited. Two whole weeks. Sometimes the Lord puts you in the express lane.

He brought Moe into my life. My love, my heart, my one and only, and the one whose absence still tears at my soul. I won't go into all the blessings she was to me because I did that in the previous book. But to say that they were abundant is insufficient.

He gave us three magnificent children. He guided me in my career to be successful and to use it as a base for standing up for my faith in Jesus Christ. He gave me opportunities to lead men's groups in churches. He brought me pastors who were also dear, dear friends.

But the reason I write this is also the most difficult to express. When Moe went home to be with the Lord, I think that is when He decided to use me instead of let me remain enmeshed in my grief. As I began to deal with, or process grief as the experts call it, I felt the need to write. I can't explain why, I just knew that I HAD to start getting it all down on paper.

By way of reports from those who have read the book, it seems to have helped those who are mourning and in need of spiritual support. That was my prayer for it, and I believe He is using the words that He gives me. Not ego here, just availability for the highest of causes.

Jill Carattini, in the RZIM publication *A Slice of Infinity*, recently wrote the following, *"For the past decade, doctors and psychologists have been taking notice of the health benefits of reflective writing. They note that wrestling with words to put your deepest thoughts into writing can lift your mind from depression, uncover wisdom within your experiences, provide insight and foster self-awareness."*

An "Aha!" moment.

Johnny Cash once said, "Being a Christian isn't for sissies. It takes a real man to live for God - a lot more than to live for the devil." I could not agree more. I was taking the easy way and it was useless. But when I surrendered, I became what I believe to be useable. Someday, I want to be able to look my Lord in the eye and hear Him say, "When I gave you the opportunity to stand for Me, you did. Well done."

"They wander on earth and live in heaven, and although they are weak, they protect the world; they taste of peace in the midst of turmoil; they are poor, and yet they have all they want. They stand in suffering and remain in joy, they appear dead to all outward sense and lead a life of faith within."

DIETRICH BONHOEFFER

Similarities

This ought to get your attention. As I was reading the Word recently, I was struck by some of the amazing similarities between Jesus, the disciples, the Apostle Paul, and me.

Now, I could leave that statement right there and you would be entirely justified in slamming the book shut and calling for a good old-fashioned book burning. But bear with me and let me explain. I'll even use the Bible to prove my points,

First, Jesus. No, I don't have a Messiah complex. Actually, there is only one legitimate comparison that can be made between the two of us. It is found in the book of Isaiah 53:2. Isaiah writes *"…He has no stately form or majesty that we should look upon Him, nor appearance that we should be attracted to Him."* In short, Jesus was not the male-model beautiful man that the movies would have you believe. He was ordinary looking in physical form, but it was His words, His wisdom, His knowledge of Scripture, His healing, His compassion, and His Godliness that made Him attractive. I only fulfill the physical mediocrity aspect of this comparison.

Before I get to the disciples, let me show my similarity to the Apostle Paul. In 1 Timothy 1:15, Paul writes, *"It is a trustworthy statement, deserving full acceptance, that Christ Jesus came into the world to save sinners, among whom I am foremost of all."* When I look back on portions of my life, I believe that I gave Paul a run for his money on that "foremost of all" ranking. There is no question about the fact that I sinned egregiously when I was younger, and we all continue to sin even today, hopefully not to those depths. But the treasure is that when we ask for forgiveness and repent, not only are we forgiven, but the Lord forgets the sin and removes them as far as "the east is from the west".

Obviously, I must deal with Thomas. We share the same name. I know, I know.

Tom Tom the Piper's son

Little Tommy Tucker

Peeping Tom

And, from the disciple, Doubting Thomas.

But my comparison with Thomas has nothing to do with doubting. My allegiance with Thomas comes from the fact that he asked the tough questions. In John 14:5, it reads, *"Thomas said to Him, "Lord we do not know where you are going, how do we know the way?"* This leads to Jesus answering with one of the most profound statements in the Bible in verse 6, *"...I am the way, and the truth, and the life; no one comes to the Father but through Me."* Like Thomas, I ask the tough questions of my students, fellow teachers, my loved ones, and especially of myself. But I also stand with Thomas when, as he saw the risen Lord, said in John 20:28, *"My Lord and my God."* Attaboy, my brother.

In John, Chapter 12*, we read of how Judas used to pilfer from the money box that was used by Jesus and the disciples for food and to help those in need. I, too, stole from the Lord when I did not tithe 10% before I got married.

When I see myself in Peter, it is not because of his famous denial. Nor is it because of his energetic if misguided temperament when he attacked the centurion. Or when Jesus had to say *"Get thee behind me, Satan"** when he wanted to go against Jesus wishes. My similarity comes in Matthew 14, starting in verse 29*. They see Jesus walking on the water and Peter wants to do it, too. Jesus invites him and once on the water, Peter becomes frightened and eventually starts sinking and cries, *"Lord, save me."** I, too, have often sought to accomplish something in a Christ-like manner only to doubt myself and begin to fail. But, like Peter, I also have Jesus to stretch out His hand and help me up.

Finally, I must mention John, This is a simple one, in John 13:23* John calls himself the one whom Jesus loved. I also claim that and know it to be true. Last year I saw a man in an airport wearing a hat which had "Jesus Loves You" written above the bill. I walked up to him, smiled and said, "Yes, Jesus loves you." I smiled, so did he, and after a pause I added, "But, I'm His favorite." As I walked away we were both laughing and he yelled out, "God bless you."

I returned the favor.

I know that John saw himself as one especially loved by Jesus, but isn't it magnificent that we all can make the same claim?

*John 12:6 *"Now he (Judas) said this, not because he was concerned about the poor, but because he was a thief, as he had the money box and he used to pilfer what was put in it."*

*Matthew 16:23 *"But He turned and said to Peter, "Get behind me Satan!..."*

*Matthew 14:29-31 *"And He said "Come!" And Peter got out of the boat, and walked on the water and came toward Jesus. But seeing the wind, he became frightened, and beginning to sink, he cried out, "Lord, save me!" And immediately Jesus took hold of his hand, and said to him, "You of little faith, why did you doubt?"*

*John 13:23 *"There was reclining on Jesus bosom one of His disciples whom Jesus loved."*

"Every book is a children's book if the kid can read."

MITCH HEDBERG

On Being a Grownup

My guardian angels have been inexhaustible. Just to name a few of the incredibly foolish, immature, and sometimes dangerous things I've done could take up an entire book on their own. Here are just a few:

- I went swimming in a waterfall fed pool in the Kaweah River in Sequoia National Park and looked up to see a mountain lion calmly watching me swim.
- I played a makeshift game of Frisbee golf, at midnight, in a darkened funeral home and, yes, there were bodies in there.
- I've driven my Harley-Davidson motorcycle at over 100 miles an hour on deserted stretches of highway.
- At the age of 71, I body surfed in La Jolla, California.
- As a youth, I challenged an entire family of five boys to a fight because they were picking on my little brother.
- I retired from one job and began another at the age of 60.

- I skied at Lake Louise, outside Banff, Alberta in Canada, when the morning temperature was 18 degrees below zero.

That should establish my credentials as being more than likely certifiably loony.

The strangest thing about all of those examples, and the multitude of others in which I engaged, is that I never had a single moment of trepidation about doing them. I wasn't even doubtful or nervous about marrying Moe on our wedding day.

What truly did frighten me, was the birth of my children. Was I competent, qualified, experienced, sufficiently stable and mature enough to bring up a child? The answer was, probably not.

But praise the Lord, I had a partner, helpmate, and guide who was a natural with our children. Moe was a magnificent mom. Thoughtful, caring, loving, watchful, protective, and every other characteristic one could desire in a mother. Despite my inadequacies, she encouraged my journey to what I hope was the successful accomplishment of fatherhood. Together we tried so hard to be godly parents.

I just wish she were here with me as I continue my excursion through the vicissitudes and marvelous blessings of being a grandfather, with another wonderful grandchild imminent. Of course I will be there for my kids and their kids. I will spoil my grandchildren as much as I'm allowed. And I will do my best to be a grandpa they will remember with love and fondness.

I will also tell them stories of their grandmother and how much she loves them, just like I'm sure their parents will tell them the same.

However, I will NOT tell them about the incidents I mentioned above. They can read it in the book when they're old enough.

*"Anger is the fluid that love bleeds
when it gets cut."*

C. S. LEWIS

The Termagant

The following story is non-fiction. It happened to me. And that's the truth.

I could see her anger a city block before I could hear it.

Stomping feet, mildly gesticulating arms, a rigid back and riveted focus were obvious to me even from that distance.

As I drew closer, I observed more details. Her appearance was almost wistfully familiar. Scuffed penny loafers, white bobby socks, a plaid skirt a bit too far below the knee to be stylish, and a long sleeved cotton sweater over a plain blouse all harkened to the late 1950s or early 1960s.

But it was the shoulder length graying hair crowning a sharply featured and lined face that betrayed a well into middle aged woman whose fashion sense had terminated, along with her innocence, in her teenage years.

The venomous hostility seen in the expressions on that face betrayed no hint of mercy. I knew that this was not an individual in a simple disagreement or argument, but a frenzied woman venting her anguished fury and hate at someone who had quite obviously grievously hurt or offended her.

While ominously pointing at the shop window, the veins on her neck stood out in violet counterpoint to her crimson flushed cheeks. The detestation etched into expression showed that evildoing had crossed a line none dare approach and that this one was extremely fortunate to be out of physical range of this potentially viciously violent and vengeful victim.

As I watched from what I thought to be a safe distance, I could hear her tirade against the offender. Names and descriptions she used on this malefactor were beyond vulgarity, not to mention biologically impossible creativity. I was glad that there were no children to hear her laundry list of obscenities that would have made the most vulgar and coarse comic blush.

After a few more moments, she finished her tirade with a phrase that, though it startled me, was logical in its summation of her emotion. Telling this person how much she loathed them, she concluded by screaming at the height of her volume and pitch that if she ever encountered this individual again, she would slowly, agonizingly and mercilessly torture them to death.

With that, she stomped away from the window still mumbling epithets and invectives. She hurried directly past me without any overt acknowledgement of my existence. Had I been directly in her path, I was certain that she would have stormed directly over me.

In a few quick jogging steps, I reached the store window. I knew that I just **had** to see the target of all of this. To see the cruel, vile monster who could cause such an eruption of wrath.

To my great surprise, not only was no one standing in the building who could be seen, but the shop was closed and the lights inside were off.

What I did see sent a chill into my soul that only time, prayer, and the arms of loved ones could begin to thaw.

For, this antique shop had only one rather large item facing out its display window toward the sidewalk……a mirror.

"But no one can tame the tongue; it is a restless evil and full of deadly poison. With it we bless our Lord and Father, and with it we curse men, who have been made in the likeness of God;"

JAMES 3:8-9

On Faith

"There's nothing like rejection to make you do an inventory of yourself."

JAMES LEE BURKE

Answers I Didn't Want

I've learned a lot of lessons about prayer through this life. Many have been tough to take.

I hate math, it is and always has been my least favorite subject. As soon as they put letters in it, instead of just numbers, they lost me. Of course, I could always do percentages since I was constantly calculating batting averages in my mind, but other than that I was, let's just say, not successful.

I remember when I was in, I believe, first grade. One night we were given a math assignment as homework. Being such a young, idealistic, and naïve boy, I prayed that God would do the homework for me and I left my BIG 25 composition book in my desk and went home. The next day, when I pulled out the notebook, I was surprised to find that God had not done the homework for me. The answer to my prayer was "No." And I couldn't explain to the teacher why I didn't have the assignment.

In my teen years, whenever I would go out for the evening, I would do something that most would find incredibly strange. As I quietly made my way to my bedroom, I would stand outside their rooms and listen to see if my Dad, Mom, and brother were still breathing. As I lay down to sleep, I would finish my prayer with, "If any of my family are going to die, please take me instead." Again, the answer was, "No." Looking back, I can be incredibly grateful for that denial.

The list of prayers to which I have received the same answer is quite long. For the Tigers to win any particular game, for me to get a date with a girl I admired from afar, to be given a good singing voice, for the destruction of my enemies, for my hairline to stop receding, and so many others are examples of these refusals on the Lord's part.

But the rejection that was the hardest to take was the one to the request I made in January of 2017. I prayed that Moe would survive the ordeal through which she, and we, were going. That some kind of healing would take place that would spare her life and send her home with me. Again, no was the answer. The result of that was the distraught rubble that was my heart.

Some could say that these prayers, some ludicrous and others deeply serious, went unanswered. That misunderstands the entire foundation of our relationship with God. He is our Father. And fathers sometimes have to say no to their children in order to spare them pain, or teach them a lesson, or provide a different way to proceed for their own benefit or for the benefit of others.

Regardless, I've never felt that my prayers have gone unanswered, just that they were declined. From my perspective of over 71 years, I can more clearly see why many of those rejections were made and the good that came from the lessons learned. Even with the loss of my love for this little while, I understand as best I can and I praise Him for caring for the both of us.

There is a scene in the Robert Duvall film titled, *The Apostle* that resonates with me. The character played by Duvall, The Apostle E. F., goes up to a bedroom in his mother's house and prays. Not your liturgical recitation, but a knockdown, drag out, argument between the character and his Lord. He pleads, he shows anger, he argues, he demands, and he finally submits. It is genuine authentic relationship being exhibited.

All I will say is, I've been there.

Soren Kierkegaard once said, *"Prayer does not change God, but it changes him who prays."* I'd add that wisdom through prayer is hard won and often excruciating and heartrending in its accomplishment. But without it, there is no victory.

> *"Christ is not valued at all, unless He is valued above all."*
>
> AUGUSTINE

The Name

Back when he was doing stand-up comedy, I had the pleasure of seeing Steve Martin in concert, twice. The first time was in a small comedy club and it was a night filled with laughter and unbridled fun. During the concert, he told one joke that truly struck home with me and I still find it to be profound.

In the story, Steve dies and, as is usual in these types of jokes, he goes to the "pearly gates" and steps up in front of St. Peter. After perusing Steve's life, Peter says, "Hmmm. Quite a few times taking the Lord's name in vain." Steve answers, "What?!? How many times? What? A million-seven? Jesus Chr…(at this point he covers his mouth with his hands)". We roared with laughter.

Unfortunately, the name Jesus Christ has become, in America, abused beyond any comprehensible notion of propriety. Just watch a movie, or a TV show, or listen to the radio. His name is used as an invective, and expletive, a vituperation, a curse, and an obscenity.

One of my favorite movies is *Trouble with the Curve* starring Clint Eastwood. As I re-watched it the other day, I was struck by the distressing use of my Lord's name. In one of the final sequences, the general manager of the team watches a young pitcher throw pitches in a tryout. After each impressive pitch, he blurts aloud, "Jesus Christ!"

I taught American history for 44 years, over 30 of them in high schools. Every year or so, I'd have a student blurt out Jesus name in class as an exclamation. At that exact moment, I would stop all that we were doing. I would address the entire class and say the following, "The name Jesus Christ is sacred to some of us in this room, including me. I will not nor will I ever allow anyone in my classroom use it as an invective." Now, let's get back to work.

Interestingly, beside the shock on some students' faces, and the smiles on others, I didn't have to deal with it again for that year because word spread.

I was at the grocery store the other day, in the self-checkout line. A man at the next kiosk from mine was having a problem with his register. Each time it didn't do what he wanted, he'd say, "Jesus Christ". And he increased in volume. Finally, as I was getting ready to leave, he bellowed "JESUS CHRIST!", to which I calmly added, "...didn't have anything to do with that machine's malfunction."

At my daughter's wedding in April of 2017, three months after the death of my wife whom I adored and loved so deeply, I was to not only speak but also to pray after my speech during the service. I proudly accepted this wonderful assignment. As I prayed before this gathering of about 200 people of various faiths I concluded, as

I always do, my invocation by saying, "I pray this in Jesus name, Amen."

Once we had all eaten our dinner and the reception celebration had begun, a middle-aged woman came up to me and introduced herself. She then told me that when I had ended my prayer, she almost shouted, "Praise the Lord!" She said that she was so happy that I was unashamed of my faith in Christ and that I would stand firm in my faith by ending the prayer in Jesus' name.

I never saw that coming and I didn't deserve the credit she gave me. We should just do what He would want us to do and never want to disappoint Him.

Let's face it. Someday, we will face Jesus Christ Himself. I sure don't want to hear about a million-seven or about my not defending and standing up for His name.

"You can't really be strong until you see a funny side to things."

KEN KESEY

Life Verses

There is a habit of mind out here in evangelical-land that everyone must have a "life verse". A verse that one memorizes and guides one's life. As if the entirety of Scripture can be condensed into one bumper-sticker sized verse.

Sorry, fellow believers, but this drives me crazy.

The verses that are most chosen are, of course, John 3:16*, John 14:6*, any portion of Psalm 23*, portions of Romans, II Thessalonians and on and on. For years I would respond with John 14:6, but I secretly wanted to say what the great writer Philip Yancey's brother would answer. He would stand and recite 1Chronicles 26:18, *"At Parbar westward, two at the causeway, and two at Parbar."* Yancey also says that if his brother were in a bad mood, he'd quote Psalm 137:9. It reads, *"Happy shall he be, that taketh and dasheth thy little ones against the stones."* Yancey's brother and I would get along just fine.

In recent years, I've changed my answer to that silly question. I say, Psalm 2, verse 4, *"He that sitteth in the heavens laughs, the Lord scoffs at them."* I love that verse for so many reasons, the first of which is that God laughs. That is so contrary to what is taught in so many churches today. He has a sense of humor. Of course he does, He made us in His own image and, Lord knows, some of us have a sense of humor.

I'm going to take you on a small trip here, but I do have a purpose. It is to lead you to another favorite verse of mine. In my last book, I talked about my grandmother's funeral and the hilarious event that occurred at that time. What I didn't write about was a further punchline from the story. So, below is the original telling and then I will add what happened after.

I've experienced laughter at some of the most inappropriate times in my life. One was at my grandmother's funeral in the hills of Kentucky. Let me tell you that my grandmother was not, there's only one way to say this-an object of the love of her grandchildren. She was a tough woman who was not affectionate. I'll leave it at that.

My several male cousins and I are genuinely hilarious, especially when we get together. At the wake for my grandmother, we were all asked to leave the room because we were telling really funny stories about each other. Well, on the day of the funeral, we had to carry my pretty large grandmother to her final resting place on a snowy side of a hill in the cemetery. We'd all been laughing together in the cars on the way there but we were holding it together during the pall bearing. That is until my one cousin slipped and started rolling down the hill. I was shaking with glee when one of my female cousins, thinking I was weeping, gently touched my arm and told me "She's in a better place".

I lost it.

Here's what happened after that disaster. The entire group of mourners, about 40 of us, went to a restaurant to eat. As you can guess, it was a loud and boisterous group where we cousins were sitting. At one point in the afternoon, my cousin who had fallen halfway down the hill, spoke up. He loudly proclaimed, "Well, you know, destiny has a way…" It was at that moment that a miracle occurred. Every one of us stopped talking. He had the undivided attention of the entire group of 40 and probably the wait staff too. I will now provide you with what he said, every syllable.

"Well, you know, destiny has a way…{absolute silence from the crowd}…I have no idea."

The only way to describe the reaction to that gem of wisdom is pure, unadulterated hilarity and ridicule. There were suggestions that we all get that printed on a business card in order to always have its genius to guide us, or perhaps a tattoo, or even have it embroidered and framed to put up in our homes right next to the "Home Sweet Home" one.

I know that God laughed, too.

So what's the additional verse about which this story always reminds me? I Peter 3:15 *"…but sanctify in your hearts Christ as Lord: being ready always to give answer to every man that asketh you a reason concerning the hope that is in you…'*(KJV)

Sound advice for everyone, especially when you're trying to be profound, or to share your faith.

There is no greater challenge to one's beliefs than to be asked the simple question, "Why?" "Because" just won't do it. When I'm asked, I have several reasons I give that are beyond the personal. For example, I mention how all 12 of the disciples went to horrible martyr's deaths proclaiming the risen Lord, including Matthias who replaced Judas. There was nothing earthly in it for them to maintain their stand, but they did so. Once someone told me that was like the 9/11 terrorists dying for their belief. But I told them that the disciples were different. They were not just operating on faith, they had actually seen the risen Lord. If that were not true, they were human after all, they would not have gone to their earthly fate as they did. They would have folded.

Another answer I use is the mathematician's proof. Of the over 61 Old Testament prophesies that Jesus fulfilled, Mathematician Peter Stoner chose a random eight of them. They were:

He was born in Bethlehem.

He was scourged at His trial.

Soldiers gambled for His clothes.

He was crucified.

A messenger was sent to prepare His way (John the Baptist).

He entered Jerusalem on a donkey.

He was betrayed by a friend and His hands were wounded.

He was betrayed for 30 pieces of silver.

So here are the odds on those eight happening to any one person. Remember that they were written a minimum of 400 years before Christ's birth. The odds on any one individual fulfilling just those eight prophesies ends up being one in ten to the 17th power, or one in one hundred quadrillion.

To picture that, here is an equivalent. Cover the earth's land mass in piles of silver dollars 120 feet high. Pick one and mark it. Bury it anywhere on the planet. Then have a previously blindfolded person find it by choosing one coin from the entire earth.

Another answer I've used is keeping a secret. Let's face it, if Jesus did not rise from the dead, over 500 people faked seeing Him and kept the secret.

Right.

For Heaven's sake, the most powerful people in government couldn't keep Watergate a secret. Someone always breaks the chain and talks. That's human nature.

I use those as my answers as to why I believe and then I get personal with my experience with the Lord in my life. I use them because some people won't initially accept a Biblical reason for faith, so I have to be ready with an earthly answer for the hope that resides in us.

It must be done with a loving heart and with humor if possible because, remember, *"He who sits in the heavens laughs…"*

*John 3:16 *"For God so loved the world that He gave His only begotten Son, that whosoever believeth in Him shall not perish, but have everlasting life."* (KJV)

*John 14:6 *"Jesus said to him, "I am the way, and the truth, and the life; no one comes to the Father but through Me."*

*Psalm 23 *"The Lord is my shepherd, I shall not want. He makes me lie down in green pastures; He leads me beside still waters. He restores my soul; He guides me in the paths of righteousness for His names sake. Even though I walk through the valley of the shadow of death, I fear no evil, for You are with me; Your rod and your staff, they comfort me. You prepare a table before me in the presence of my enemies; You have anointed my head with oil; my cup overflows. Surely goodness and lovingkindness will follow me all the days of my life, And I will dwell in the house of the Lord forever.*

*"The pain of parting is nothing to the
joy of meeting again."*

CHARLES DICKENS

A Batting Order of Heroes

I'm going to steal an idea from the writings of Mitch Albom. He has written a book titled *The Five People You Meet in Heaven.* When I first saw that title, it sparked a cavalcade of thoughts and, if I'm truly honest, wishes. We know we shall be with the Lord for eternity and that allows us plenty of time in which to get to meet people whom we've always harbored a desire to meet or have met.

That being the case, here are a nine of mine. A batting order, so to speak. Of course, these would be the ones with whom I'd love to have conversation AFTER having rejoiced with family, friends, relatives and other loved ones for centuries. Since the Lord will be constantly with us, He goes without saying. This is my batting order of some of the first earthly ones I want to look up.

1. *John the Baptist.* How can one not want to meet the one who heralded the Messiah? The one who knew Jesus before he was even born (look it up in Luke 1: 41-44)? The one who spoke ultimate truth to power at the expense of his life? The one of whom Jesus said no greater

one born of woman has arisen than he, John the Baptist? Easy choice.

2. *Tyrus Raymond Cobb.* Yes, smart alecks, he will be there. The greatest baseball player of all time and the one after whom I named my son. I'd just love to sit and listen to him talk about hitting. For decades.

3. *Billy Graham.* His wisdom, his faith, his dedication, his moral righteousness, were and are all standards to which all of us can aspire. I want to meet the man who accomplished so much for the Lord.

4. *Dietrich Bonhoeffer.* The man who stood up to ultimate earthly evil and whose writings have inspired me so much. His courage and steadfastness to his faith inspire awe and admiration.

5. *Theodore Roosevelt.* The man who lived crowded hours. He packed so much brilliant achievement into just almost 60 years. He's been a hero of mine from the moment I encountered him in study, but for one more important reason. TR wasn't just a great man, he was a great father who loved and was adored by his children.

6. *Mary Magdalene.* I want to hear her full story, not the suppositions of those who think they know her biography. I also want to hear her describe how she felt and what she saw when she was the first to encounter the angel and the risen Lord.

7. *C. S. Lewis.* I want to thank him for *A Grief Observed* and *Mere Christianity*. There really aren't two more impactful books, other than Scripture, in my life. And, if I'm being truthful here, I'd also love to sit and listen to him tell stories.

8. *Winston Churchill.* Anyone who loves studying the past would want to listen to the stories that man would have to tell. Since he was the one who stood up to Hitler and inspired a nation and the world to defeat the terror of Nazism, he would be one who would teach such a lesson in history.

9. *Margaret Thatcher.* The "Iron Lady" had more courage and plain gumption that all of her peers in world leadership, matched only by her friend Ronald Reagan. She was an inspiration to all women and especially to all freedom loving people of the world.

On the bench and ready to play: William F. Buckley, Jr., Ronald Reagan, Shoeless Joe Jackson, Alice Roosevelt Longworth, Pistol Pete Maravich, Elizabeth I, Alexander Hamilton, Salvador Dali, and so many others.

And I'm bringing Moe with me.

So who's on your wish list?

Teaching History

"Good news is rare these days and every glittering ounce of it should be cherished and hoarded…"

HUNTER S. THOMPSON

Go Ahead and Try to Put a Price on It

One does not go into the field of teaching for money. That would be akin to becoming a pearl diver in the Sahara Desert. It is just not going to happen.

Teaching does, however, bequeath wonderful gifts to those who practice it. I have been blessed with so many intangible gifts from my 44 years as a teacher, it boggles my mind. Recently I've gotten emails from former students telling me about how I touched their lives and inspired them to achieve great goals in their lives. One became a poet, another a professor, a few in government, many went into teaching, some were inspired to take stands for their Christian faith as I had, and some wanted to thank me for providing them with the memories of classes they cherished. The list could go on and on. One of my favorites told me that my class could be described in three adjectives; rigorous, supportive, and fun.

I simply want to mention five of the most wonderful gifts that I received as a teacher, out of so many, and to prove to you that this noble profession is so priceless.

One of the gifts is camaraderie. As an AP teacher, I have been one of the exam leaders at the annual AP US History Exam Reading. It is an arduous week of reading student essays from all across the country and scoring them. Many of the teachers who attend this reading are leaders in the profession of teaching. And some, like yours truly, are a bit looney.

One of the most common errors made by students at the reading is chronological reasoning. They simply put events or people in the wrong era. One year, there was a question we were scoring about the Puritans. A fellow reader named John Adams, how appropriate, came over to my table and offered a bet on which one of us would get a reference furthest out of the Puritan era. I agreed to the bet at which time he produced an essay booklet from his back pocket and let me read, "The Puritans had troubles with the Quakers. Richard Nixon was a Quaker."

He smirked.

I told him there was still time for me to win this wager, a dinner, and that I would not give up. Two days later, I went to his table and told him that I look forward to my free dinner. I produced the essay which had in it, "The Puritans adhered to their faith like Obi Wan Kenobi adhered to the Force." I said, "Long ago and far away, I can't lose." I will never know who the kid who wrote that was, but I owe him or her a dinner.

The second gift is humor. There are three requirements for being a successful teacher. First, love your subject matter. Kids will know in a minute if you don't. Second is have a sense of humor. And third is teach for an audience of One. If you please the Lord, nothing else matters.

Here are two examples of wonderful student humor. When I was student teaching in a middle school, I said, "Today I've discussed big business and tomorrow I'm going into labor." I froze. I was a student teacher. Quickly I turned to the blackboard and the bell rescued me. The students said nothing.

The next day, I walked into my classroom to find it completely decorated in pink and blue, baby shower presents all over the place, a cake, and a card that said, "Congratulations on your most unusual baby." And all of this from 8th graders.

As I've mentioned before, chronological reasoning is a national deficit in history students. One of the most egregious errors involves Rosa Parks. Poor Rosa appears in essays covering all eras. Puritan era, Roaring 20s, the Civil War and Reconstruction, you name it. I always told my students about this and one particular student would always put her name in every essay he wrote for me, crossed out, just to get me. Well, at the end of the year I gave his class a take-home writing assignment and told them all, while looking at him, that if anyone wrote the name Rosa Parks anywhere on the essay, I would lower the grade dramatically.

The next day, this young man brought in his assignment and slipped it into the folder in which I was collecting the work. I told him to freeze, and I reached in for the essay he had hidden in the pile. He had not written Rosa Parks name on the assignment. Instead, he had printed it on a scanned picture of Rosa Parks. I love that kid.

A third gift I received was treasure. I taught for 38 years in a majority/minority district. I loved those young people.

When they found out that I was retiring from the district, my last classes there surprised me. I was summoned to the auditorium over the PA. When I went in, the place was completely dark. As I walked further in, the curtains on the stage parted and all of my students from that year and the previous year, were there. They had cake, refreshments, and they gave me a gift. It was a beautiful clock with the following inscribed on it, "You Will Always Be Part of Our History". I was, and am, so deeply touched by that gesture.

The fourth gift was grace. For the last three years that I taught at the Thomas Jefferson High School for Science and Technology in Alexandria, VA, I had a problem. I had retired in Michigan after 38 years of teaching there, and brought my family with me to VA. After three years, my youngest daughter moved back to Michigan and for those three years, my wife and I lived apart during the school year so that we would not lie on our taxes. Our accountant said that to claim our home as a residence, we had to be living in it.

I would make the nine hour drive as often as I could and would always go home for holidays and the summer. But, we were apart and it hurt.

My students at TJ were aware of my situation, though I didn't tell them all of the details.

In December of 2010, I was asked by a wonderful assistant principal if I would help her supervise an activity in the cafeteria during an activity period. I said that of course I would. She and I went to the cafeteria that afternoon and she opened the door before I could get to it. When I got in, I was greeted by over 100 of the students I had taught the previous year. There was a huge banner that said, "We love you Mr. Sleete", a poster board with the same message and all of their senior pictures attached, and food and cake to feed an army. I was so deeply moved, and I thanked them sincerely.

Then, one of the girls came up to me and said that they had gotten me a gift. I said that they didn't have to do that. She said, "Its right over there by the door." I looked and in walked my wife. These kids had collected money and purchased a flight ticket for my wife to come to VA to be with me at Christmas. For the first time in my professional life, I was speechless. And stunned. And overwhelmed. What a magnificent gesture by students who were formerly in my class, for whom there was no possible gain to be had.

But that doesn't end the story. Once I had hugged all of them, one of the young ladies came up to me and said that there was a problem. I told her that no matter how short they were on the cost of the ticket, I would make up the difference. She laughed and said, "No, Mr. Sleete, that isn't it. You see, we did this on

Facebook because we know you're not on it and we could get away with it. Well, we had so many donations, even from students you've never had, we have $100 left over. So, here. Go have a nice dinner with your wife." And she handed me the money.

Gifts I did not deserve so selflessly provided by the Class of 2011, whom I will NEVER forget.

The last gift I received was by far the most important, significant, and valuable I have and will ever receive. It was love.

In early 1977, a wonderful young girl in my American History class came up to me after class one day and said, "You should go out with my sister." I thanked her for the thought.

She then said, "She's an art teacher." Having just escaped from having to go out with an art teacher who told me she couldn't go out until she talked to her guru about it, I got ready to decline the offer.

Then came the clincher. My student said, "My sister has a Corvette." I asked, "What's her number?

So, on Friday, May 13, 1977, Moe and I went out on a blind date to please her little sister. And, on July 8, 1978, we married. My student had given me the open door to true and lasting love by simply saying that she thought we'd be a good couple.

So, go ahead, try to put a monetary value on that.

"History is a guide to navigation in perilous times. History is who we are and why we are the way we are."

DAVID MCCULLOUGH

"You don't hate history. You hate the way it was taught to you in high school."

STEPHEN AMBROSE

Yeah, but...

One of my favorite historians is the late Barbara Tuchman. When asked how history should be taught, she gave a two word answer, *"Tell stories"*. Here's one of mine.

What I am about to write will alienate some of my readers. It will do so because they might jump to conclusions about me and about my philosophy of history, let alone their conclusions about my political leanings. Rest assured that what you are about to read is in no way political, it is from the heart and about a subject I love, American history. Even more, the subject is the teaching, and lack of appreciation, of American history pervading our culture.

Most importantly, it is about teachers.

One of my former students, an African-American gentleman, was recently engaged in a discussion on Facebook on the relevance or need for Black History Month. I quote his entry here in order to provide evidence for those who do not know me, of who I am and was as a teacher.

"I have to say that I was fortunate to have Mr. Sleete as my Honors and AP US History teacher while at Southfield-Lathrup. We never had to formally talk about black history, because it was actually included in the curriculum. If he was teaching about the 1720s, we learned about ALL Americans in the 1720s. No one was excluded.

It was also an interesting dynamic having a staunch conservative teaching a bunch of liberal kids who were largely minorities. There were some fun moments in that class, and I enjoyed every second. I'm sure that most people who were in his class feel the same way. If American History were taught in the same fashion as he taught it, we wouldn't need Black History Month, but unfortunately…it isn't."

In the last few years, I have encountered an approach to teaching that I believe is destructive. I believe that our job as educators is to inform and teach students HOW to think, not WHAT to think. It is that position that has been eroded to the point that to embrace it is to be considered a dinosaur.

When pointing out any evils in the world that need or needed confronting, this new cadre of teachers engages in the most disingenuous form of proselytizing. It is the "Yeah, but…" approach. No matter the villainy, they feel compelled to present an example of an equally odious event in American history to prove that we are "just as bad". Fabricated equivalence.

This past summer I overheard a teacher in one of my workshops, during group work, inform others about a terrible event of racist violence in the deep south that he tells his students about in order to try to demonstrate some form of equivalence between the United States and the ISIS tactic of burning or beheading their enemies. One vile event as opposed to a state philosophy and accepted practice. And no one disagreed with the absurdity of his position, they all just sat there like an "amen chorus."

The more I have observed and listened, the more I know that the prevailing viewpoint of so many teachers is to denigrate our past and our standing as a nation, at the cost of ignoring or twisting the truth of the past in order to fit it into their standpoint.

I know that we live in what some have called a "post truth culture". To that I say, "What the heck is that supposed to mean?" How can anyone say there is no truth since saying so belies their declaration? To avow there is no truth means that the very statement is false. My former teacher, Margaret Hollowell, had it right when she told me to always ask, *"What are the facts?"*

I'll get off the soapbox by stating what I always thought was obvious. Teach American history to the youth, warts and all. Tell the whole story, not just the self-flagellating guilt trip. Did we have slavery? Yep. Did we fight our bloodiest war to end it? Without a doubt. Has there been de facto and de jure prejudice in our country? Certainly. Have we waged continual attempts to legally erase them? Undoubtedly. Is our government perfect? Of course not. But, as Churchill once said, *"No one pretends that democracy is perfect or all-wise. Indeed it has been said that democracy is the worst form of Government except for all those other forms that have been tried from time to time…"*

James Mattis, the former Secretary of Defense, said it brilliantly. *"If you read enough biography and history, you learn about how people have dealt successfully or unsuccessfully with similar situations or patterns in the past. It doesn't give you a template of answers, but it does help you refine the questions you have to ask yourself."*

To those who do not allow the positive about our past into their teaching, the ones who shout down or demean opposing viewpoints, the ones who won't listen to, or learn from the past, the ones who are compelled to make EVERY event or situation political, who think they are on the "right side of history" (whatever the heck that is or how it can be determined in the present), I can only close with the following. ***Ignorantia historia non excusat.*** (Ignorance of history is no excuse.) It is there for exploration and learning, not for cherry picking events just to make one's point and jam them down student's throats performing propagandizing, not real teaching. Let the students think for themselves.

Though I don't want to be repetitious, I will conclude with the answer I always gave to student who asked how it was I could be an enthusiastic in my teaching and love of history. I said, "I teach for an audience of One, and if I please Him, I know I've done well. How could I possibly give less than my best effort?"

*"Those who don't know history are
doomed to repeat it."*

EDMUND BURKE

> *"Those who do know history are condemned to watch those who don't screw things up."*
>
> THOMAS F. SLEETE

Yeah, but...Part Two

Previously I advocated taking a stand on the factual truth of American history with students and letting them come to their own conclusions. But, I now must ask, how can I do less with Jesus Christ?

Upon encountering a Christian who is unashamed of his or her faith, the "yeah, but" crowd has their ready ammunition. They will trot out the Inquisition, the crimes of some in the Roman Catholic priesthood, the public sins of some televangelists, the profit motive preaching of some other clergy who preach false doctrine of faith for monetary profit, and others.

These arguments are, by their very nature, fallacious. They are not about Jesus Christ, they are the practices and crimes of humans hiding behind the name of the Lord. Believe me, they will answer for these, but they have nothing, and I mean nothing, to do with the historical and living Son of God.

Another trope they have in hand is the Old Testament. For example, they say, "so you believe we should stone disobedient children, your Bible says to do that"? Of course, that ignores the fact that by His own words, Jesus said that He was the fulfillment of the old covenant and He was the new covenant.

"But", they proclaim, "your faith is so repulsive in its exclusivity." We claim that Jesus is the way to God. Excuse me, but doesn't every faith make that claim? And don't the atheists make the obverse claim by stating that there is no God? Or that there is no truth?

The science argument also has its dramatic flaws, too many to elaborate here. Instead I will recommend the writings of Lee Strobel, Michael J. Behe, Phillip E. Johnson, Hugh Ross, Michael Dembski, and many others. They make the conclusive case for the compatibility of Christianity and science. In addition, isn't it interesting that historically until our current age of rampant disbelief, the greatest scientists believed in God? Charles Darwin, Isaac Newton, and Albert Einstein to name just three.

One of the worst, is the claim that Christians are judgmental. Well, let's face it, many of us are. But the truth of the matter is, He isn't. He is the one who told the religious leaders that only the one without sin could condemn the woman caught in adultery. Though He was without sin, neither did He condemn her but He said for her to go and sin no more. He was the one who begged God to forgive the ones killing Him for they were sinning out of ignorance. If only those who make this claim would truly and sincerely read the Sermon on the Mount, or just read those words written in red in some editions of the Bible, they'd get to know the real Jesus Christ.

That is our job, to lead them to Him. We are to set an example following the truth He lived in order to provide the facts by which those outside of the faith can come to their conclusions. In His prayers and relationship with His Heavenly Father, Jesus inhaled the presence of God. And in His life and ministry to and with others, He exhaled the Will of God. That is an example to which we all must strive to achieve.

That does not include responding to those who attack our belief in kind. Author Jim Carattini, in response to an article by Sam Harris titled *On the Freedom to Offend an Imaginary God*, wrote, *"There is no doubt that Jesus frustrated more than a few scribes; he was fairly harsh on the rich, and he responded angrily to the commercialization of the temple. Yet while these are the scenes we might summon to substantiate hostile words when the God we love is debased with insult, Harris is right. Jesus told anyone who would listen that the greatest commandment is to love God with everything that is in us, and the second greatest commandment is to love our neighbors as we would ourselves."*

In doing so, we must keep in mind what Jesus said in Matthew 5: 11-12, *"Blessed are you when people insult you, persecute you, and falsely say all kinds of evil against you because of me. Rejoice and be glad, because great is your reward in heaven, for in the same way they persecuted the prophets who were before you."*

Other Observations

"The most valuable of talents is that of never using two words where one will do."

THOMAS JEFFERSON

A Counterintuitively Elaborated Digression on Brevity

We talk too much. And too loudly, without listening. I blame Maury Povich, Jerry Springer, and Bravo TV for part of this, along with our ever growing self-absorption. Through their "entertainments" people have been subliminally trained to believe that talking over individuals, being louder and more vulgar, and never listening, is the way to make a point.

When I was a kid, we had a bar soap around the house, called Lava. The ad for it read, "Lava, with Pumice." It was the grittiest soap one can possibly imagine. Oh, it got the dirt and grime off all right, along with a couple of layers of skin. But heaven help you if you tried to use it on your face. What passes for discussion or dialogue today I find to be the verbal equivalent of good old Lava Soap.

But herein I'd like to make a point that just a very few words, assuredly written or spoken, can have far greater emphasis and impact.

I am not trying to make a political point here. All segments of the political spectrum are guilty of the coarsening of the culture. No one side's hands are clean.

The brilliant author Norman Maclean, in his masterpiece *A River Runs Through It*, told of how his father, a pastor, taught him to be a good writer. Each time he would polish a piece of prose or analysis, he would present it to his father. After his father read it, he inevitably would say, "It's good. Now make it shorter."

Elmore Leonard told prospective writers, "...when you write, leave out all the parts that readers skip. Louise Brooks wrote that "Writing is one percent inspiration and ninety-nine percent elimination." And once, famously, Pascal wrote, "I have made this letter longer because I have not had the time to make it shorter."

There have been magnificent examples of brevity in speech which have successfully captured the moment, the point, and the audience. Such as the previously quoted statement by the late historian Barbara Tuchman.

William F. Buckley, Jr., was asked why his vision of utopia had never occurred on earth. He replied, "Invincible ignorance." Andrew Jackson, when told that the Supreme Court, led by John Marshall, had ruled against him in a case dealing with Indian Removal said, "John Marshall has made his decision, now let him enforce it." And Stalin, when told the Pope wanted Catholic oppression stopped in the Soviet Union stated, "The Pope? How many divisions does he have?" And Ronald Reagan, when asked whether or not he trusted the Russians in negotiations said, "Trust, but verify."

My parents said a simple four word phrase each time I would leave the house. Going to school, out with friends, or just to hang around, they said, "Remember who you are." I've never forgotten it. They wanted me to be myself and no one else because they knew who I was at my core. A speech from them would have sounded like the Charlie Brown adult sound, "Waah Waah", but the brevity of that valediction had a far greater impact.

It is my belief that if we could turn down the cacophony of today's over saturated world, we'd have a far greater impact with our words. Facebook, Twitter, Snapchat, the 24/7 news cycle, TV shows with people hollering so much they need subtitles for anyone to understand what is being said; these all contribute. And I am fully aware that I am a delusional dinosaur who wants less of what society desires more, but I know that understanding, empathy and sympathy would increase if it were to happen.

We have the ultimate teacher in God's Word. I'll leave you with just two examples, though a thorough reading of the Sermon on the Mount in Matthew delivers a treasure trove of brief verses with incredible impact. These two examples encapsulate such profundity by their command and their context.

The first is the shortest, in English, in Scripture. As Jesus approached the newly occupied grave of his dear friend Lazarus, dead just four days, John 11:35 says, *"Jesus wept."* He shows us his love, compassion, empathy, and his sharing of our sorrows when we also lose a loved one. He went through it just as we have, or will.

Then He demonstrates His power and dominion over death by saying, *"Lazarus, come forth."* And out of the grave he came. Back to life. The first demonstration of resurrection.

The second, and last of the brief verses comes from 1Thessalonians 5:16, the shortest verse in the original Greek, in Scripture. *"Rejoice always."* Now that is a really tough one. Paul, who wrote it, knew of the sufferings of the church in Thessalonica since he had just been there ministering to them. But with this simple phrase, he exhorted them to keep their eyes on the ultimate prize.

I for one among a very few, resolve to ironically increase my brevity in speech in the hope that the impact or thoughts behind what I have to say will be comprehended more clearly.

"Don't be so humble. You're not that great."

GOLDA MEIR

Stooping to Conquer

Moe had a great line about one of my heroes, William F. Buckley, Jr. When I asked her what she thought he'd be like as a president, she said he would never run. I asked why and she replied, "It would be beneath him."

I laughed out loud.

Unfortunately, today we live in a society in which condescension is both common place and adored. Coastal elites demean the people of "Fly-over America." Those from the heartland look down on the "Ivory tower PC police". A president who uses Twitter for adolescent rants about anyone who dares to oppose him. Another former president who informs those who do not support what he supports that they are on the "wrong side of history." (How could he become as prescient as to know what will happen in the future?)

So many exhibit smirking disdain at others. The coarsened culture metastasizes. No side in the culture wars is immune from criticism on this issue. None get off scot free.

Scripture tells us what the Lord thinks of all this posturing, preening, arrogance, contempt, patronizing, and haughtiness. Psalm 37:13 says, *"The Lord laughs at him for He sees his day is coming."*

So what does that mean? It is explained in 1Corinthians 1:27, *"...but God has chosen the foolish things of the world to shame the wise, and God has chosen the weak things of the world to shame the things which are strong..."*

Our job is not to lord it over others whom we perceive as our lesser, but to interact with love and provide an example of how one should live. But never let it be said that they weren't provided with an example of Christ-like attitude while they still had a chance on this earth. Because we, the "foolish", will provide it.

"It takes less time to do a thing right than to explain why you did it wrong."

HENRY WADSWORTH LONGFELLOW

Semantics

My Dad, a Baptist pastor loved to tell the following story. It seems that a young couple was going to get married in the church. As part of the program, the pastor had chosen a scripture verse as the basis of his message before the vows. He chose 1John 4:18, *"There is no fear in love; but perfect love casts out fear, because fear involves punishment, and the one who fears is not perfected in love."*

Unfortunately, the person who typed up the program wrote that the message would be based on John 4:18, which reads, *"...for you have had five husbands, and the one whom you now have is not your husband; this you have said truly."* After relating this, my Dad would make his point that almost is never enough.

We are surrounded by slight inaccuracies that are accepted and tolerated as truth. Just think of the statements that are attributed to the Bible which are nowhere to be found in it. Such as:

God helps those who help themselves.

To thine own self be true.

Love the sinner, hate the sin.

Cleanliness is next to Godliness.

And on and on. I once alienated the husband of a friend of my wife's by correcting him on a Bible quote. On one visit to their home, he brought out a sheet of uncirculated dollar bills that he had purchased at the Bureau of Printing and Engraving in Washington, DC, and had had framed. He showed it to us and called it quite proudly, "The Root of All Evil". I said, "Unfortunately, that isn't the full quote. It really says, "The love of money is the root of all evil."

He didn't speak to me for the rest of the night.

So why do I bring this up? The reason is three bumper stickers that I've recently seen. They've made me want to pull the person over and tell them how wrong their message is on the back of their car.

The first I saw in Kentucky on the back of a truck. It read, "If It Ain't King James, It Ain't Bible". Wow, so much to say. For example, which King James? 1611 or 1739? If he had said 1611, I'd have bet him his truck that he's never even seen that edition since it is in sometimes incomprehensible old English. I'd also recommend *The King James Controversy* by James R. White. That book puts to rest the objections of the KJV Only crowd.

The second sticker said, "Jesus is My Co-Pilot", I'd love make a simple comment. I'd just say, "Seriously, dude. Jesus is your ***Co-Pilot***? Change seats, man."

This last one is a quote that I've seen attributed to both John F. Kennedy and also to Bill Gates' mother. It generally reads, "*From those to whom much is given, much is expected.*" All I should say is, "Luke 12:48*. It's in the Bible. Check it out."

---

*Luke 12:48 "…From everyone who has been given much, much will be required…"

On Reading

"I just downloaded eleven hundred books onto my Kindle and now I can't lift it."

STEVE MARTIN

Top Twenty-One

Theodore Roosevelt said it best when he wrote, "*A thorough knowledge of the Bible is worth more than a college education.*" There is no way I can top that. I must admit though that I have encountered books along the way which have helped enlighten me into not only the Word, but also into my relationship with God, Jesus Christ, and the Holy Spirit. So, here are my top twenty-one Christian books which I say, through life's experience, are invaluable for one's bookshelf. When I mention Bibles, I refer to the study Bible format. My personal favorite is the one by Charles Ryrie.

The Holy Bible - King James Version. The poetry of the language used and the beauty of its diction make it so worthwhile.

The Holy Bible - New American Standard Bible Version. This is the most accurate to the original texts as one can find.

The Holy Bible - New International Version. I recommend this because most churches in evangelical circles use it.

Mere Christianity - by C. S. Lewis. When it comes to apologetics, this is the pinnace of achievement.

Jesus among Other Gods - by Ravi Zacharias. Speaking of comparative religions and apologetics, another classic.

What the Bible is All About - by Henrietta Mears. The best introduction to the Bible.

Evidence that Demands a Verdict - by Josh McDowell. When it comes to defending the validity of scripture, this is the strongest.

The Cost of Discipleship - by Dietrich Bonhoeffer. A classic that demonstrates our relationship with the Lord Jesus.

Knowing God - by J. I Packer. If you *think* you know Him, you more than likely don't or haven't read this book.

The Screwtape Letters - by C. S. Lewis. All about temptation in an entertaining and incredibly enlightening way.

My Utmost for His Highest - by Oswald Chambers. The devotional up to which all others look.

How Should We Then Live? - by Francis Schaeffer. This shows how to live in today's declining and coarsening culture.

The Pursuit of God - by A. W. Tozer. For those who wish to go deep in their knowledge of God and the grace which He bestows.

Lectures to My Students - by Charles Haddon Spurgeon. These are priceless gems showing not only his love of the Lord and his knowledge of Scripture, but also his sense of humor. A great teacher.

Where is God When it Hurts? - by Philip Yancey. This, along with *A Grief Observed* by C. S. Lewis, helped me when I lost the love of my life, my wife.

Foxe's Book of Martyrs. Delivers what our forefathers in the faith endured. Incredible.

What's So Amazing about Grace? - by Philip Yancey. Such a powerful and practical book about Grace, what it is and why we so don't deserve it.

Your God is Too Small - by J. B. Phillips. A wonderful book that expands our knowledge and perception of the Lord.

Pilgrim's Progress - by John Bunyan. The classic. If you haven't read it, you should.

How to Be a Perfect Christian: Your Comprehensive Guide to Flawless Spiritual Living - by The Babylon Bee. This satire is priceless and, honestly, I laughed out loud while reading this look at modern day evangelical churches by members of same.

Finally, get yourself a good Bible Commentary. I recommend the one by Matthew Henry or by John MacArthur.

"Picking five favorite books is like picking the five body parts you'd most like not to lose."

NEIL GAIMAN

"Always read something that will make you look good if you die in the middle of it."

P. J. O'ROURKE

The Joy of Reading

For all of our years together, I was Moe's "literary acquisitioner". I would scour libraries, bookstores, magazine articles, and other sources to try to find novels and non-fiction I thought she'd like. I have to admit that I was pretty good at it with a success rate of over 90%. She was always grateful for what I provided and we loved to talk about and critique them.

I know that she has much better reading material in Paradise, but I so miss sharing the privilege of providing the books and spending time with her. Just the two of us, sharing something we both loved.

By now, you will not be surprised by the following statement, I was a strange kid. Painfully shy, I would use my sense of humor to protect me. In high school, I was the class clown. I fought shyness for years, with little success until college helped me start to come out from behind my protective barriers.

To prove my strangeness, I remember when I was first asked if I had a favorite author. I was somewhere around ten or eleven. My answer stunned the adult who asked me the question because I answered, "Edgar Allen Poe". And I was not kidding. I LOVED

Poe. Any list of my favorite fiction books I've read, always begins with "Anything by Poe."

Today, I have a lot of writers I enjoy. A few favorite Christian writers are Ravi Zacharias, Randy Alcorn, Philip Yancey, C. S. Lewis, Dietrich Bonhoeffer, Anne Graham Lotz, and Lee Strobel.

With those disclaimers, I offer thirteen (plus) of my favorite novels with a sentence or two description for each. I do so that when you are looking for a good book for the beach or vacation, these are ones I thoroughly enjoyed and highly recommend.

Fair warning: this is a secular list. They are in no particular order, just how I remember them. Since I have already listed the books about faith that I have found to be irreplaceable, this list is for fun.

Boy's Life - by Robert McCammon. This story is a mystical mystery, adventuresome, character driven, and a masterpiece. My wife and I read it to all of our kids and they loved it. Once you read, it just remember the following name, Nemo Curliss.

Poe Must Die - by Marc Olden. Poe, bare-knuckles boxer Pierce James Figg, and the most evil villain I've ever encountered in literature.

The Ghosts of Belfast - by Stuart Neville. An ex-IRA hitman is confronted by the ghosts of those he's killed and they want vengeance on those who ordered their demise.

Lucifer's Hammer - by Larry Niven and Jerry Pournelle. A gigantic comet approaches and hits the earth. Great characters and a truly scary outcome.

The Cosgrove Report - by G. J. A. O'Toole. A detective investigates Lincoln's assassination with newly discovered files.

Time and Again - by Jack Finney. A classic of time travel and it has the most perfect ending of any novel I've ever read.

Lonesome Dove - by Larry McMurtry. The best western ever with characters you never forget. Or want to.

A Prayer for Owen Meany - by John Irving. I didn't really care about the parts that didn't have Owen, but those that did were wonderful.

The Veritas Conflict - by Shaunti Feldhan. I'll just say that she nails the college experience and what a Christian student must endure.

Deadline - by Randy Alcorn. A moving and thought provoking novel about death and what is after.

Fielder's Choice - by Rick Norman. An American ballplayer held in a WW II Japanese concentration camp teaches the chief guard's little son how to play baseball.

Shoeless Joe - by W. P. Kinsella. The book on which my favorite movie, *Field of Dreams*, is based. And it is a great book.

A Wolf Story - by James Byron Huggins. A story for young and old about a wolf, a heroic rabbit, and true heroism.

Okay, once I got going, I couldn't stop.

Additions, war novels: *Catch-22* by Joseph Heller, *The Things They Carried* by Tim O'Brien, *Johnny Got His Gun* by Dalton Trumbo, and *Killer Angels* by Michael Shaara.

Six more novels I loved and then I'll stop. *One Flew Over the Cuckoo's Nest* by Ken Kesey, *For Love of the Game* by Michael Shaara, *The Sunbird* by Wilbur Smith, *84, Charing Cross Road* by Helene Hanff, *A God Against the Gods* and *Return to Thebes* by Allen Drury.

Some favorite historians to read: Doris Kearns Goodwin, Barbara Tuchman, Amity Shlaes, David McCullough, William Manchester, Edmund Morris, Stephen Ambrose, and David Pietrusza.

Favorite commentators whose work I have enjoyed: Tom Wolfe, William F. Buckley, Jr., Peggy Noonan, Joe Queenan, and P. J. O'Rourke.

On Grieving

PART TWO

"I'm still runnin' against the wind."

BOB SEGER

Compare and Contrast

It's December and, of course, getting close to Christmas. As I've started decorating parts of the house with ornaments, lights, and artificial trees, the whole process reminds me of Moe. How she would take hours to make it all look just right, Beautiful and meaningful.

Even harder on me, I find her handwriting on the boxes of ornaments identifying what is in each box, some with humorous references. Naturally, my missing her is brought more to the poignant present and that pain in my heart amplifies.

As I've written before, this is not a negative thing. I have so many positive and loving memories on which to fall back and contemplate, I am not one who should complain. Nevertheless, that hole in my soul is still there and it longs for her.

This brings me to my final point. Why is it that some people try to make grieving a compare and contrast escapade? I was recently asked how I'd reply if someone had the temerity to ask me why it is that I am still in the process of grief since it has been almost two years since I lost her.

It is confession time. I answered in the best way I could, with fierce honesty. What I said would terminate the conversation and I doubt whether the questioner and I would ever deliberate on the topic again. From depths of my soul, and as truthfully as humanly possible, I simply would say, "I guess that you haven't loved as deeply and in the same way that I did. It produces a loss that cannot be trivialized or be ruled by a stopwatch."

So I will go on tolerating those hurtful feelings of loss and longing that life presents, whenever they occur. I will do this knowing how much treasure I had while she was here and how much the richer I will be when we meet again in the Lord's presence.

And I promise I will work on a more subtle rejoinder should this kind of accusation occur.

"I'd kill for a Nobel Peace Prize."

STEVEN WRIGHT

Sadness and Irony

When Moe was finally taken to the Cardiac Intensive Care Unit of the hospital, we encountered a large and rather unfriendly family. My kids named them the Magillicuttys for no apparent reason, it just sounded right for them.

The family was there because one of their members, a man appearing to be in his early thirties, was in a dire situation due to an opioid overdose. Surrounded by machines, he was also on a respirator.

Within a day of our arrival, the young man died. But the family refused to let the hospital take him off the respirator until relatives arrived from out of state, the next day, so that they could say their goodbyes.

The staff gently tried to let them know that he was brain dead and would not hear them, but the family was adamant. So they waited until late the next day before they allowed him to be taken off the machines.

I was truly saddened by this and I thank the Lord to this day that Moe always knew that we loved her and in life we told her so constantly. In that hospital room it was our mantra. Even if she had died alone, not one of us would have felt any guilt over the fact that we hadn't made her know of our love. We didn't wait until it was too late.

On a somewhat lighter note, the dictionary defines irony as an event that seems deliberately contrary to what one expects, and is often amusing as a result. The night before Moe passed into the Lord's presence, a different family took up residence in the waiting area outside the CICU. There were young and old and I'd guess there were at least ten of them. To the teens, this seemed to be a time to play video games and slouch around taking up at least two seats per person.

That evening the father, I assume, of the younger ones, brought dinner to the waiting room. So what did he feel was an appropriate feast in a hospital? A "Crave Case" of White Castle hamburgers and cheeseburgers with a dozen orders of fries. A "Crave Case" contains 30 of those hamburgers. If you've never seen one, they are nicknamed sliders and are greasy to say the least. The "beef" in them is of minimal proportions and if it didn't have cheese, a greasy bun, pickles, onions, mustard and ketchup on it, and were eaten alone, no one would consume it due to the fact that it does not taste like any beef you've had before. I believe that all of the accoutrements are to mask that "flavor".

I won't even begin to describe the smell of this cornucopia of cholesterol.

The irony here is that he felt that while waiting outside a unit in which people were often dying of heart ailments, it was appropriate to have his family gorge on the type of food that had perhaps helped hasten their loved one to the ward.

It is strange that the memory of these people stands out to me. I guess the mind and memory are pretty tricky in how they shelve incidents in the data banks while one is going through a trauma that beggars them into insignificance.

"I love you in a place where there's no space or time."

LEON RUSSELL

In and Out of my Mind

The brain is a pretty tricky machine. Among its myriad duties, it provides one with thoughts and dreams. Most are relevant to life and others make one want to ask one's consciousness, "What the heck was that all about?"

In the immediate aftermath of Moe's passing, I had vibrant and, frankly, awful dreams and thoughts that kept recurring. I was right back in the Cardiac Intensive Care Unit, with her, watching the whole two weeks of hell that culminated with my reliving her passing. Miserable does not begin to define that time.

As time has passed, those dreams and thoughts have become few and far between. I don't feel guilt over trying to push them into my subconscious because it is not an act of abandoning her but is rather an effort to subsume the miserable and replace it with the positive.

On occasion, other weird dreams have taken the place of those wretched ones. Dreams in which I am back teaching, God know where, and can't seem to get things organized to do my job. Or ones in which I am trying to get someplace, again I don't know where, and am not able to do so for a myriad of illogical or peculiar reasons. Those are just two of many types of dreams with which I've dealt. I'd say I am going crazy, but most who know me would tell you I've already reached that plateau.

I was going to worry about all of that, but I came to a conclusion. I think that my brain is letting off steam and pressure by "entertaining" my subconscious and keeping it busy. By doing that, it sets up a firewall to block out the dismal thoughts of reality from that time.

One thing has remained a constant in these types of dreams. Not every time, but quite often, Moe enters the dream to lend a hand or provide guidance. My brain knows what a positive influence she was and is on me and it inserts her into that kind of role. Never negative, always positive and loving. And she ALWAYS stretches out her hand to touch and hold mine. Always loving, just like I am always loving her. And will till the end of time.

In other words, we are and will always be connected. I love that.

"Those are my principles, and if you don't like them...well I have others."

GROUCHO MARX

Thoughtful, Knowledgeable, Listeners

This will be marked by its brevity and plain-spoken construction. I've had a rough go of it recently. The totality of the circumstances have severely upset my status quo. They include physical ailments, psychological turbulence, and seeming instability in my grasp of who and what I am. In order to deal with them, I've had to step outside of my tendencies.

Outside of the physical, I truly believe that the tide of grief has come back in at the most inopportune time. (You might ask what time is opportune and for that I have no answer). So, I decided to first do something about my health issues. For this reason, and at my daughter's prodding, I went to a specialist and he found not only the source of my problems, but also others that have more possibly severe complications. The good news is that these are ultimately controllable and I praise the Lord that I went to the physician before the worst happened.

As for the rational and spiritual upheavals, I went to see a Christian, faith-based counselor. Stan is wise, intent, intelligent, perceptive, and supportive. He and I have no holds barred talks of such depth and, quite frankly, they have greatly ameliorated my situation. I am definitely not a group therapy kind of guy, but these few one on one talks are beneficial. I tell you this in case you are one who needs to unburden yourself to another who can facilitate your progress through heartache.

Lastly, I again had it out with the Lord. Alone in my house, I talked to God with honesty, sincerity, passion, and unfortunately anger. There was, indeed, some shouting involved. I made my case and He has begun to show me the answers to some of my pleas while leaving others to eventuality. Not because of my anger, but because He loves me and I finally asked. I must say that unburdening myself to, and being honest with, my Heavenly Father has been spiritually uplifting.

There. No charge for these three prescriptions.

*"I know your image of me is what I
hoped to be."*

LEON RUSSELL

Trying

Moe left me a poem among the other things she wrote to me. It is by the 17th Century American poet, Anne Bradstreet and it is titled, *To My Dear and Loving Husband*. I won't provide it here, but I heartily recommend that you look it up online and read it. You will see how blessed I was and am to have been her love.

And it will give men a goal to which they ought to aspire.

But, as Leon Russell wrote and sang, I hope that I am what she saw me to be.

Lord knows, I'm still trying to be that man.

In doing so, I have made a decision about the way in which I still deal with the grief of losing her. I refuse to be that guy, the one lying in the ditch by the emotional road of life, ensnared by self-pity and heartbreak.

These pangs of sorrow still strike even after a year and ten months since she went home to be with the Lord. They can hit when a certain song is heard, or I see something that reminds me of her and us, or in dreams, or when someone else brings her up in conversation, and in a multitude of other ways.

Instead of wallowing in the morass of defeatism, I will now choose victory. In my mind, and aloud if necessary, I will address these paroxysms of lamentation with the word, "Hallelujah."

Hallelujah because I have so many positive memories of her and what we were, and did, and shared. Praise Him because he allowed us over 38 years to build these memories and feelings. And most of all, glory to our Savior whose promise is that we shall meet again in eternity.

Out of the ditch and on the road to becoming what her image of me is and was.

> *"I never could stand losing. Second place didn't interest me. I had a fire in my belly."*
>
> TY COBB

Sorry For You

You never got to know her, my wife Moe, who passed away on January 20, 2017.

You didn't see her the way I did when we first met. When she opened the door to her apartment, I was stunned. A man of many words, I was at a loss. All I could say was, "Pretty girl." Speaking of losers, I was one. Yet, she saw the humor in it.

You missed out on the most beautiful moments I ever had watching the woman I love give birth to my children. All three.

You didn't see her on our wedding day. Or hear her Uncle Pat ask me if I meant all I said in the service. I said, "Of course I did." He replied, "We'll see in five years." Well Pat, old boy, we made it over 38 years.

You didn't get to play softball at Softball City, in a tournament in November, when it was snowing for our 11 PM game, and hear the only fan in the stands cheering for her Tom.

You didn't get to hold hands with her all of the time. Walking, in stores or church, even at home.

You didn't get to benefit of her incredibly accurate instincts. She called it her Holy Spirit Radar. It happened when she would know if a person wasn't trustworthy almost instantaneously.

You missed out on how we shared the total enjoyment of just being together. The two of us. We didn't need anyone else. Ever.

You didn't get to experience her incredible selflessness.

Your taste buds didn't get to experience her incredibly delicious cooking.

You didn't get your wedding ring made, by her, from the same mold as hers.

You weren't there when we were counseled by Father Prus at Shrine of the Little Flower. He and I really hit it off. But when it came time for the forms to be signed, you didn't get to hear her tell him that we would not sign them if they said we'd raise our children Catholic We would only sign if it said we'd raise them as Christians. He approved it on the spot.

You didn't get to water baptize her, one of the most magnificent honors of my life.

You didn't get to see and hear her depths of compassion and empathy. When Moe was pregnant with our first child in 1984, in July of that year she asked me to take her to Washington, D. C. on a two person tour. I had been a tour guide in D. C. before we met and I was thrilled to take her. As I mentioned, it was July, hot, and she was eight months pregnant. But I had such a wonderful time showing her the city I love. When we got to the Vietnam War Memorial, we walked slowly down the path looking at all of the names inscribed there who gave their last full measure of devotion. And I noticed that she was crying. I said that it is powerful because it is our generation but she said that was not the reason she was crying, it was because every name on those walls had a mother and that mother had lost her child. Such power and grace in that observation.

You didn't get to share in some of the quotes from books she read, that she loved and shared with me. Like these about life's end:

> *"For what is family, anyway, but the people you pull closest and refuse to let go."*

> *"Do you know that there's a halfway world between each ending and each new beginning? It's called the hurting time. Give yourself the time you need. Some thresholds are too wide to be taken in one stride."*

> *"The death of our loved ones is merely a threshold between ending and a new beginning."*

> *"Keep your eyes closed and your head down (at a funeral). Do you know why? Respect? There's more to it. At the funeral of a good person, the sky fills with angels. But we don't look up in case we don't see them."*

> *"All at once everything had meaning and I wasn't scared of dying. I have given life, and pain was the path to joy."*

> "Be the kind of woman that when your feet hit the floor each morning, the Devil says, "Oh crap, she's up."

> "Death less feared gives more life."

> "The will of God will never take you where the grace of God can't sustain you."

> "A single person is missing yet the whole world is empty."

> "When I get to heaven, if they ask, I'll say I'm with you."

> "You can give without loving, but you cannot love without giving."

> "Meus Bonus Amicus Deus Consultrix" (My good friend God provides)."

> "I'll lose everything, but I'll never let go of your hand."

But here is where you are a winner. You didn't have to be the one holding her hand when she went home to be with the Lord. That is where I momentarily became the biggest loser ever, and suffered the darkest hours of my life.

And after that moment, I was touched by the fact that the Lord Jesus had snatched that loss right out of Death's grip and promised me that we would be together again.

So, I win. And it is my sincere prayer that you will be joining us there in Heaven, so that I can introduce her to you.

> *"I'm a member of the 1960's generation.*
> *We didn't have any wisdom."*

P. J. O'ROURKE

I Can Just Hear Her

I have to admit that at 7:27pm on January 20th, 2017, (as I mentioned previously) I could have been found in a ditch by the side of life's toll road of grief. Devastated and shattered, I began my life without Moe, frankly not knowing which way to turn, how to proceed, or just who the heck I now was. In those initial moments and hours, I subsisted in a vortex of emotion and bereavement.

Being the blessed man that I am, there were others who were there with me. My Lord and Savior, my children, my brother, my sister-in-law, my pastors, and my friends. Dozens of others sent their prayers and well wishes. And, somehow, I made it through to this point.

At this Christmas season, I feel even more close to Moe than at any time since she's been gone. It's funny, but I can almost hear her at times. For example, when I go to throw out something that was hers and it is no longer of any use she would say, *"It's about time you got rid of that"*. Or when I agonized about tearing down the deck that she designed she'd say, *"It's not me, Tom, it's just a thing"*. Then, too, when I profoundly need her to be here with me to provide her wisdom and insight she would say, *"I'm so sorry that you have to do this alone."*

Most importantly, though, when I long for her touch and to just be with her, I know that she would say, and is saying, *"Soon, Tom, soon."*

I decided to do something a little different the other day, and I will never know if it was even worth the effort until that day I go home to be with my Lord. But I did it anyway.

I've had some physical setbacks recently and it's been a bit difficult to navigate my way to some form of healing. I had a dark time in my mind. So I went to a location that Moe and I shared and I opened my heart to God, aloud. At one or two points it was a strident conversation on my part. I told him what I thought and needed. We have a relationship, He and I, and I can be fully honest and myself with Him. Not profane, but overwhelmingly emphatic.

It was then I asked Him to do something for me. I said, if it were within His will, would he pass along a message from me to Moe? I didn't expect an answer from her, I just wanted to say some things. I then verbalized what was on my heart and that I needed to elaborate. Now, I don't know if she's a part of the "great cloud of witnesses" that Scripture mentions are the ones who observe what I and we do, but I definitely felt better after I said what I needed to say.

I hope she got the message. Perhaps it was just venting. But even if she didn't, I know that she is well aware of how much I loved and still love her, because I told her so in this life.

And that is a sure knowledge I will take into eternity.

I believe Honore de Balzac summed it up well when he wrote, *"True love is eternal, infinite, and always like itself. It is equal and pure, without violent demonstrations: It is seen with white hairs and is always young in the heart."*

"Death cannot kill what never dies."

WILLIAM PENN

Rounding Third at Full Speed

Since I've now passed the second anniversary of Moe's passing, I will conclude with these thoughts. Ever since I wrote the first book, I believe the Lord has been using me. Me, most likely the most imperfect person on earth I would choose to do His work. In 2018 alone:

- I spoke at Grace Bible Church in Charleston, WV, to a group of wonderful people who are grieving. (Thank you, Christy Day, for the invitation.)
- I've been approached to facilitate a group of widows and widowers in my new church, starting in January.
- He has provided me with the impetus to witness to a dear friend of Moe's who is just so close to accepting Christ as his savior.
- He gave me the opportunity to provide insight into how I've handled grief to a pastor who is in mourning of a different type, but mourning nevertheless.

- I've had scores of people read the book and the feedback has been humbling. The reviews on Amazon have been astounding. It has accomplished its three goals: to honor God, to honor Moe, and to be a source of help to others grieving.
- I was made aware of how the book actually helped a young lady get off suicide watch after the passing of her grandfather.

That was just a partial list of the doors that the Lord has slammed open.

It is always said that before God uses someone, He first breaks them. Well, Lord, mission accomplished.

But from here on out, I want to be a man after His own heart, doing His will, and providing comfort to all whom I can reach.

www.ingramcontent.com/pod-product-compliance
Lightning Source LLC
Chambersburg PA
CBHW051344040426
42453CB00007B/397